THE OPPORTUNITY MINDSET

NO IS NEVER AN ANSWER

A True Story of a Young Prodigy's Passion, Perseverance and Record-Breaking Success

PRITISH A R

INDIA • SINGAPORE • MALAYSIA

Copyright © Pritish A R 2024
All Rights Reserved.

ISBN 979-8-89363-409-9

This book has been published with all efforts taken to make the material error-free after the consent of the author. However, the author and the publisher do not assume and hereby disclaim any liability to any party for any loss, damage, or disruption caused by errors or omissions, whether such errors or omissions result from negligence, accident, or any other cause.

While every effort has been made to avoid any mistake or omission, this publication is being sold on the condition and understanding that neither the author nor the publishers or printers would be liable in any manner to any person by reason of any mistake or omission in this publication or for any action taken or omitted to be taken or advice rendered or accepted on the basis of this work. For any defect in printing or binding the publishers will be liable only to replace the defective copy by another copy of this work then available.

Contents

CHAPTER 1

A Musical Journey Begins

1.1   A Melodic Bond: The Womb and Beyond

My musical journey began long before I even took my first breath. My Mum, a passionate music lover, often talks about the special connection we shared while she was pregnant with me. She would lovingly refer to me as her little prince and eagerly awaited my arrival. As she went about her daily life, Mum would lose herself in music, finding comfort and inspiration in the melodies that surrounded her.

It was during these moments of musical joy that Mum first noticed my unique response to two particular songs. When she played the first song, I would become incredibly active, moving and kicking with an energy that seemed to match the rhythm. It was like the music sparked something within me, filling me with indescribable happiness. On the other hand, when Mum played the second song, a sense of calm would wash over me, and I would gently sway to the soothing notes, eventually drifting off into a peaceful sleep.

Mum found great delight in this extraordinary bond we shared, and she would often play these songs to interact with me, much like the stories of the prince from Indian mythology, responding to his mother's stories while in the womb. It became our special language, a way for us to communicate and connect on a deep level.

As Mum's pregnancy progressed, there were times when she couldn't feel my movements as frequently, which would fill her with concern. In those moments, she would turn to our special song – the one that always triggered my active response. The moment the music began, I would start moving again, reassuring her that I was okay. It was a beautiful reminder of the power of music and the strong bond we had already formed.

On the flip side, there were also times when my movements became too intense, causing Mum discomfort. Whenever this happened, she would play the soothing song, and almost instantly, I would settle down, as if the melody was a gentle lullaby, easing me into a state of relaxation.

After I was born, our musical connection only grew stronger. As a baby, I was prone to crying and fussiness, but Mum quickly discovered that the same song that calmed me in the womb had an almost magical effect on me. Whenever I was upset, she would play that special tune, and I would immediately stop crying, my little eyes closing as I drifted off into a peaceful sleep.

This became our go-to solution for any situation where I needed comfort or soothing. During long car rides, like our three-hour trips from Sydney to Canberra, Mum and Dad would have the song ready to play at a moment's notice. If I started crying or becoming restless, they would put the song on repeat, and I would instantly relax, remaining calm and content throughout the journey.

As I grew older, my love for music only deepened. Mum, recognising my natural fascination, made sure to surround me with a variety of musical toys and experiences. She would borrow musical toys from toy libraries and purchase ones that caught my eye, encouraging me to explore the world of sound and melody.

I clearly remember how determined I was about making my parents sit down and listen to the music I created with these toys. I needed them to be a part of my musical journey, to witness the joy and excitement I felt when I played. If they didn't give me their full attention, I would become upset and start crying. I would only stop crying when they showed interest and appreciation for my little performances.

> *From the womb to my earliest memories, music has been my constant companion, guiding me through the highs and lows of life. It's incredible to think that my story began with a simple melody, a loving mother, and an unbreakable bond that would shape the course of my entire life.*

Looking back, I now understand that music was never just a passing phase or a simple hobby for me. It was an essential part of my being, woven into the very fabric of my existence from the moment I was in my mother's womb. Those early experiences, the songs that soothed me and the ones that energised me, were the foundation upon which my musical journey would be built.

1.2   Nurturing the Musical Spark

As I grew older, my parents, especially my Mum, played an important role in nurturing my musical talents and interests. They created a home environment that was filled with music, exposing me to a wide array of genres and styles from a very young age.

Mum, a firm believer in the power of music and its ability to shape young minds, drew inspiration from the research she had come across. Studies showed that babies are born with an incredible capacity for learning, including the ability to absorb and understand multiple languages. Mum took this concept and applied it to music, recognising that if children are taught in a way that resonates with their interests and abilities, they can achieve remarkable things.

"When you can learn complex languages, why not music?" Mum would often say, her eyes sparkling with enthusiasm. "It's all possible if we provide the right environment and guidance."

Mum's approach to parenting and nurturing my musical journey was rooted in this philosophy. She believed that every child has unique talents and passions waiting to be discovered and nurtured. By providing me with the right tools, support, and freedom to explore my interests, she knew that I could unlock my full potential.

One of the key principles Mum instilled in me from a very young age was the importance of giving my all to whatever I chose to pursue. "Whatever we do in life," she would say, "we must put in 100% energy, effort, and enjoyment, and do it right." This mantra became the guiding light of my musical journey, pushing me to always strive for excellence and find joy in the process.

Mum went above and beyond to create a home environment that supported my musical growth. She would take me to playgroups where I could interact with other children and engage in musical activities. Together, we would sing songs, dance to different rhythms, and explore the world of sound through various instruments and games.

At home, music was a constant presence. From the moment I woke up to the time I went to bed, there was always a melody playing in the background. In the mornings, Mum would put on devotional songs, filling the house with a sense of peace and spiritual connection. As the day progressed, she would switch to movie soundtracks, classical compositions, and popular albums from different eras and cultures.

This diverse musical exposure had a profound impact on my developing tastes and interests. I found myself drawn to the vast array of sounds and rhythms, eager to explore and understand the details of each genre. Mum's carefully selected playlist opened my mind to the vast possibilities of musical expression and ignited a fire within me to learn more.

One of my favourite memories from this time was exploring my musical toys. I had a variety of them that made sounds and played melodies. I would spend hours immersed in the world of these toys, creating my little tunes and rhythms. It filled me with a sense of joy and wonder, and I could easily lose myself in the magic of making music. These early experiences with musical toys further fuelled my fascination with sounds and melodies, setting the stage for my growing passion for music.

1.3   Confronting Age-Related Challenges

When I was almost five, Mum felt that it was the perfect time for me to start learning a musical instrument. She understood that this was a crucial age for developing skills and wanted to give me every opportunity to discover my true passion.

As I started on my journey to pursue music, I quickly realised that the path ahead would not be without its hurdles. One of the first I faced was the age-related scepticism from music teachers and schools. Many of them believed that at the tender age of five, I was simply too young to begin learning an instrument which was considered quite demanding.

I remember the disappointment that I felt every time a teacher or school turned us away, stating my age as the primary reason. They would say things like, "Kids can't learn at that age. It's a waste of time," or "Come back when he's older, maybe seven or eight." These rejections were like tiny pinpricks to my budding passion, but they never managed to crush my enthusiasm entirely.

Mum, being the constant support system she has always been, refused to let these bumps stop us from our mission. She firmly believed that age was just a number and that with the right guidance and support, any child could excel in their chosen vision. Mum would always reassure me, saying, "Don't worry, my love. We'll find the perfect place for you, where your talents will be nurtured and celebrated."

Her words were like a comforting hug to my young heart, easing the sting of rejection and fuelling my determination to prove the doubters wrong. Hand in hand, we kept going, visiting one music school after another, hoping to find a teacher who would see beyond my age and recognise the potential that lay within.

During this time, Mum never lost hope or allowed frustration to cloud her judgement. She approached each new prospect with the same level of enthusiasm and optimism, always ready to advocate for my dreams. Her firm belief in me was a constant source of strength, reminding me that no matter how many times we were turned away, we would eventually find the right path.

Looking back, I realise that those early rejections were not just hardships to conquer but also valuable lessons in my ability to stay strong and not give up. They taught me that following one's passion often requires facing adversity head-on and that true success lies in the ability to pick oneself up after each knock-back and keep moving forward.

> *Age is just a number, and passion knows no bounds. The challenges we face in chasing our dreams are not roadblocks but rather stepping stones to greatness. It is through adversity that we discover the true depths of our strength of our positivity and confidence.*

As we continued our search, Mum and I had many heartfelt conversations about the importance of following my dreams and never giving up, even in the face of difficulties. She would often share stories of famous musicians and artists who had faced similar roadblocks in their early years but had gone on to achieve great things through sheer determination and hard work.

These stories became my bedtime lullabies, filling my young mind with visions of a future where I, too, could handle any obstacle and make my mark on the world through music. They instilled in me a deep sense of purpose and a belief that with hard work and a supportive family by my side, nothing was impossible.

1.4   The Mobile Music Classroom

My first introduction to formal music lessons came when I was in kindergarten. A pamphlet arrived from my school one day, promoting a music bus – a mobile music school that offered lessons for young children. It was the only place that would accept students my age, and even then, only for keyboard lessons.

Excited by the prospect of learning music, Mum enrolled me in the music bus classes. The bus would come to my school, and the lessons took place during lunchtime. I had to skip my regular lunch and playtime with my classmates to attend the classes, but it didn't bother me. I was thrilled to be learning music.

However, Mum wasn't entirely satisfied with this arrangement. She felt that I shouldn't have to miss out on important things like lunch and socialising with friends to learn an instrument. She believed that learning music should be a joyful and enriching experience, not one that came at the cost of other essential aspects of my development.

Despite her reservations, Mum allowed me to continue with the music bus lessons for a few months. The music bus classes were held in a small, cramped space inside the bus, with all instruments being taught simultaneously. It was more of an introductory play space rather than a structured learning environment. Despite the limitations, it was during these classes that I first laid eyes on the drums and had the opportunity to try them out for a few minutes, sparking my interest in the instrument, but I was only allowed to take keyboard lessons.

As time went on, Mum noticed that I wasn't making progress. The lessons lacked depth, and the constant turnover of teachers made it difficult for me to establish a consistent learning experience. Mum firmly believed that whatever we pursued in life, we should do it with 100%

effort and dedication. She didn't want me to approach music half-heartedly or simply for the sake of it.

After much consideration, Mum decided to discontinue my lessons with the music bus. She realised that for me to truly excel in music, I needed a more focused, dedicated, and stable learning environment. Although short-lived, this experience with the music bus ignited my passion for learning an instrument and laid the foundation for the incredible opportunities that would soon come my way.

Looking back, I am grateful for Mum's wisdom and foresight in recognising that the music bus, while a fun introduction to music, was not the ideal setting for nurturing my true potential. Her decision to seek out a more suitable learning environment set the stage for the extraordinary musical journey that was awaiting me, one that would shape my life in ways I could never have imagined.

CHAPTER 2

Overcoming Obstacles and Finding the Right Path

2.1   The Drum Set That Almost Wasn't

After my brief encounter with the drums during the music bus experience, I was truly fascinated. The power and rhythm of the drums had ignited a passion within me that I couldn't ignore. Determined to pursue this newfound love, Mum and I set out to find a music school that would nurture my talent and provide me with the guidance I needed to learn an instrument.

We explored various options together, from singing and dancing to playing different instruments. I quickly realised that while I enjoyed listening to others sing and watching people dance, I didn't feel a strong pull towards those particular art forms. Mum, ever attentive to my interests, took note of my fascination and arranged for me to attend trial classes at a local music school. Our search led us to a local music school that offered drum lessons along with other instruments.

Excited by the prospect of finally learning to play an instrument, I attended a trial class. I took the trial lessons for guitar, drums, and piano. However, the moment I laid eyes on a drum set, something within me clicked. I felt like a magnetic force drawing me towards the power and rhythm of the drums.

I still remember the excitement that ran through my body as I sat behind the drum kit, holding the drumsticks in my tiny hands. As I struck the drums and cymbals, creating a loud noise, I felt a sense of pure joy and liberation wash over me.

After the trial classes, Mum asked me to take two weeks to think about my decision on which instrument to pursue. She wanted me to be sure that this was something I truly wanted, not just a passing fancy. Mum encouraged me to write down my thoughts, both positive and negative, in a notebook, and to consider why I felt drawn to the drums.

I took Mum's advice to heart and spent the next two weeks reflecting on my experiences. I would sit quietly, replaying the memories of the trial classes in my mind, trying to put into words what I felt when I played the drums. It was a profound exercise for a five-year-old, but Mum's guidance and belief in my ability to make informed decisions gave me the confidence to explore my feelings deeply.

When the two weeks were up, Mum and I sat down for a heartfelt conversation. She asked me once again why I wanted to learn the drums, and I replied with the innocence and conviction of a child, "No matter how many times you ask, I like drums." Mum, however, wasn't satisfied with this answer. She gently probed further, asking me to dig deeper and provide a more thoughtful explanation.

I was puzzled and a bit frustrated at first, not understanding why my simple declaration of love for the drums wasn't enough. But Mum, with her infinite wisdom and patience, helped me see that true passion is rooted in understanding and self-reflection. She asked me questions that challenged me to think beyond the surface level, to consider what it was about the drums that resonated with me on a deeper level.

As we talked, something shifted within me. I began to articulate feelings and thoughts I hadn't fully grasped before. And then, in a moment of clarity, I said, "I feel that drumkit is the right instrument for me because I want to use both my hands and my feet. I don't like the idea of keeping any part of my body idle while playing music."

Mum's face lit up with pride and amazement. She was thrilled not only by my decision but also by the level of self-reflection and self-awareness I had demonstrated at such a young age. She told me that she believed with all her heart that I would excel at playing the drums because it came from a place of true passion and understanding.

However, our journey to getting my first drum set was not simple. When we went to enrol me in lessons, the teacher informed us that we would need to buy a drum kit for me to practice at home. Mum, who had always been a strong advocate for doing things wholeheartedly, agreed without hesitation. She knew that having an instrument to practice regularly was essential for my growth and development as a musician.

But Dad had some concerns. He worried that I was too young to take on such a physically demanding instrument and that the size of the drum set might be too overwhelming for my small frame. I still remember standing next to a full-size drum kit in the store, feeling tiny in comparison, and seeing the concern in Dad's eyes.

Mum, being the incredible pillar of support she has always been, sensed Dad's reservations and took him aside for a heartfelt conversation. With patience and understanding, she addressed each of his concerns, reassuring him that we would face any tough situations together as a family. She reminded him that this was my choice, born out of genuine passion and that it was their duty as parents to support and encourage me to go after my dreams.

As Mum spoke, I could see the hesitation in Dad's eyes slowly melt away, replaced by a flicker of understanding and acceptance. He may not have been fully convinced, but he trusted Mum's judgement and recognised the importance of allowing me to follow my heart.

With a heavy sigh and a nod, Dad gave his blessing for me to start drum lessons. Mum's strong belief in me and her ability to advocate for my passions had once again paved the way for me to begin a new chapter in my musical journey.

As I sat behind my very own drum set for the first time, I felt a sense of belonging. The weight of the drumsticks in my hands, the cool sound of the electronic drum pads beneath my sticks, and the anticipation of the journey ahead filled me with a joy I had never known before.

Looking back, I realise that this moment was a turning point in my life. It was the beginning of a path that would lead me to discover my true calling and to inspire others through the power of music.

But at that time, all I knew was the pure, unadulterated happiness that came from doing something I loved with all my heart. As I struck the first beat on my drum set, I knew that I had found my place in the world, a place where I could express myself freely and create something beautiful.

Little did I know that this was just the first step in a remarkable journey that would test my determination, push me to my limits, and ultimately shape me into the person and musician I am today. With the support of my incredible parents and the fire of passion burning brightly within me, I was ready to face whatever was coming my way.

"*All she wanted was for the decision to come from within me, not influenced by anyone else. I was excited to join the drum class and little did I know that this was just the start of an incredible adventure that would shape my life in ways I never could have imagined.*" - *Pritish*

2.2 Nurturing My Passion at My First Music School

Energised by the trial class experience and confident in my decision to pursue drumming, my parents enrolled me in the local music school that had welcomed me with open arms. The teachers there recognised my potential and enthusiasm for learning the drums, and I felt a sense of belonging from the very first lesson.

The instructors at this school were patient and supportive, taking the time to understand my unique learning style and adapting their teaching methods accordingly. They celebrated my age as an asset, surprised at the speed with which I absorbed new concepts and techniques. Under their guidance, I began to flourish, my skills growing by leaps and bounds with each passing week.

As I progressed through my lessons, I found myself eagerly awaiting each new session as an opportunity to learn. The basic notes, patterns, and grooves that had once seemed so scary became second nature to me. I felt a sense of pride and accomplishment as I watched my hard work pay off.

One of the highlights of my time at this school was the annual end-of-year concert, where students had the chance to showcase their progress and perform for an audience of family, friends, and fellow music lovers. I still remember the exhilaration that coursed through my veins as I took to the stage for the first time, my tiny hands gripping the drumsticks with a mixture of nerves and excitement.

As I began to play, the world around me faded away, and I lost myself in the rhythm and the joy of playing music.

I could feel the energy of the audience, their applause and cheers fuelling my confidence and pushing me on to give my all. When the performance ended, I was met with a sea of smiling faces and proud embraces from my parents, a moment that will forever be engraved in my memory as one of the greatest achievements of my young life.

However, as time passed, we noticed certain limitations in the teaching approach at this school. While the instructors were kind and supportive, they seemed to have a fixed approach that didn't allow for much flexibility or individualised attention. I found myself craving more challenges, eager to push the boundaries of what I could achieve with the drums.

Moreover, we encountered some inconsistencies in the teaching staff. I had a new teacher every 2 weeks at one stage. The constant change of instructors made it difficult for me to form a consistent learning experience and build a strong foundation. Mum, who believed in the importance of having a dedicated teacher who could track my progress and provide personalised guidance, grew increasingly concerned about this issue.

When Mum asked the school about my progress and the next steps in my drumming journey, she often received vague or unsatisfactory answers. The teachers seemed to lack a clear roadmap for my development, and their responses left us feeling uncertain about the direction of my musical education.

It was during this time that we first learned about the AMEB grading exams, a globally recognised certification programme in Australia that would provide me with a structured framework for learning and achievement. My parents and I were excited by the prospect of working towards these milestones, seeing them as a way to track my progress and set meaningful goals for my drumming journey.

To make matters worse, when Mum inquired about the possibility of preparing for the grade exams, we were met with resistance. The instructors explained that they didn't believe in grading exams for drums and that it was mainly for piano. No one takes grading exams in Australia, and they primarily focus on teaching the basics and helping students enjoy playing the drums. They believed that taking up formal certifications at such a young age was unnecessary and could potentially hinder my natural love for the instrument.

Both Mum and Dad did not like this approach and felt that the grading exams would provide me with a sense of direction and purpose in my drumming journey. We believed that with the right support and guidance, I could balance the joy of playing with the discipline and structure of formal training.

Despite the positive aspects of my time at this school, such as the nurturing environment and the opportunity to perform, we realised that it was time to explore other options for my musical education. Mum, ever adaptive to my needs and aspirations, understood that while this school had been a wonderful starting point, it was essential for me to continue growing and evolving as a musician, even if that meant seeking out new opportunities elsewhere.

2.3 Exploring Different Learning Environments

After our experience with the first music school, we decided to explore other learning environments that might better suit my needs and aspirations as a young drummer. One such place was a music school that offered a unique combination of group performance-based lessons and individual instruction.

The group performances immediately caught my attention. They consisted of a full band setup, with a drummer, guitarist, singer, keyboardist, and bassist, all working together under the guidance of a teacher. This collaborative environment provided me with valuable insights into how bands function and the importance of communication and teamwork in playing music. I enjoyed the opportunity to play alongside other young musicians, feeding off their energy and enthusiasm as we learned to navigate the complexities of playing together.

In addition to the group classes, I also received individual lessons at this school. These one-on-one sessions focused on the fundamentals of drumming, including basic techniques, grooves, and rhythms. While I appreciated the personalised attention and the chance to hone my skills, I soon found myself craving a more structured and comprehensive approach to my drumming education.

As I progressed in my lessons, Mum and I began to inquire about the possibility of preparing for the grading exams. However, when we raised the idea with the instructors, we were met with hesitation. They explained that their primary focus was on performances through which they fostered a love for playing the drums rather than encouraging formal certifications.

Furthermore, we noticed that the individual lessons lacked the structure and consistency we were seeking. Though the problem of changing teachers was repeated here as well. Even though it was not as frequent as in the previous school, it still made it challenging for me to build a strong foundation and progress steadily in my drumming skills.

While we respected their philosophy and appreciated the emphasis on enjoyment and passion, Mum couldn't shake the feeling that we needed something more. We believed that with the right guidance and support, I could balance the joy of playing with the discipline and challenges of formal training, ultimately unlocking my full potential as a drummer.

As we reflected on our experiences at this school, we realised that, despite the many positive aspects, such as the group performance opportunities and the focus on individual instruction, it wasn't quite the perfect fit for my long-term goals and aspirations. We knew that to truly thrive and reach my full potential, I needed a learning environment that would fully support my desire for structured learning and formal qualifications.

With this realisation, Mum and I made the difficult decision to discontinue my lessons at this school and restart our search for the ideal music school and teacher. We knew that the right mentor could make all the difference in my musical journey, providing the guidance, support, and inspiration I needed to achieve my dreams. And so, armed with a clearer understanding of what we were looking for, we pressed on, ready to face everything that was approaching.

Looking back, I am grateful for the experiences I had at this school. While it may not have been the perfect fit for my long-term goals, it taught me valuable lessons about the importance of collaboration, communication, and the joy of making music with others. It also helped me to clarify my priorities and aspirations as a young musician, setting the stage for the next phase of my journey – the quest for the perfect teacher.

2.4   The Quest for the Perfect Teacher

Armed with a clear vision of what we were looking for, we began our search in earnest. Mum spent countless hours researching music schools, reading reviews, and reaching out to industry professionals for recommendations. She was determined to find a teacher who not only possessed exceptional skills and knowledge but also could connect with me on a personal level and understand my unique needs and goals.

However, finding a teacher who specialised in coaching for the drums grading proved to be more challenging than we had anticipated. Many of the instructors we approached were unfamiliar with the programme or lacked the necessary qualifications to guide me through the exams. Others simply didn't have the passion or enthusiasm we were looking for, viewing teaching as just another job rather than a true calling.

Undeterred by these constraints, Mum and I pressed on, our resolve growing stronger with each passing day. We knew that somewhere out there, the perfect teacher was waiting to be found, someone who would not only recognise my potential but also have the skills and experience to help me soar to new heights.

As our search continued, I began to develop a clearer understanding of the qualities that set a truly great teacher apart. It wasn't just about technical proficiency or impressive credentials; it was about the ability to connect on a human level, to inspire and motivate, and to create a learning environment that fostered creativity, curiosity, and a deep love for music.

For now, it is sufficient to say that we emerged from this challenging period stronger, wiser, and more determined than ever to chase our dreams and make our mark on the world. We had learned that the path to greatness is seldom easy, but that with strong resolve, faith, and an unwavering commitment to one's passions, there is no obstacle too great to conquer.

In the end, our quest for the perfect teacher would lead us to some of the most remarkable individuals I have ever had the privilege of knowing – mentors who would not only transform my drumming abilities but also leave an indelible mark on my heart and soul. But those stories are for another chapter, a testimony to the incredible power of the teacher-student bond and the transformative impact it can have on a young life.

And so, with hearts full of hope and minds full of possibilities, we pressed on, ready to accept whatever was awaiting. Little did we know then just how incredible the journey would be, or how much music would come to shape the course of my life in ways we could never have imagined. But one thing was certain – we were ready for anything, and we would face it all together.

CHAPTER 3

Perseverance and Progress

3.1 Exploring Indian Music and Drumming Independently

After discontinuing my lessons at the previous music school, I found myself at a crossroads, eager to continue my musical journey but lacking the proper guidance and support. Not letting this stumbling block stop me, I decided to take matters into my own hands and explore the world of music independently, with a particular focus on Indian music and drumming, continuing to practise every day what I learned over the past years.

I had always been drawn to the rich and diverse sounds of Indian music, captivated by the complex rhythms and melodies that seemed to speak directly to my soul. Growing up in a household where music was a constant companion, I was exposed to a wide range of Indian genres, from the devotional hymns that filled our mornings to the lively beats of film songs in most Indian languages that filled our evenings.

Now, with a new sense of purpose and determination, I immersed myself in the world of Indian music, spending countless hours listening to recordings, trying to understand the complex patterns and grooves, and attempting to replicate them on my drum set.

Armed with my trusty headphones and a strong passion, I would sit for hours on end, listening intently to the music, my fingers tapping along to the beat. I would pay close attention to the subtle details and variations in the rhythms, trying to understand the complexities of each genre and style.

Then, filled with inspiration and eager to put my new knowledge into practice, I would rush to my drum set, ready to translate what I had heard into my playing. I would experiment with different techniques and styles, trying to capture the essence of the music I had just listened to.

However, without proper guidance and feedback, I often found myself struggling to accurately replicate the sounds I had fallen in love with. There were times when I would feel frustrated and discouraged, my efforts to master the details of Indian drumming on my own seeming to fall short.

But I refused to let these difficult situations discourage me. I knew that my passion for drumming and my love for Indian music would guide me through this challenging period. I continued to practice tirelessly, putting my heart and soul into every beat, determined to make progress, no matter how small. I would spend hours practising my skills and experimenting with different rhythms and patterns. My family, ever supportive of my musical journey, would often find me lost in my world, the sound of my drumming filling the house.

There were moments of frustration, of course, when a particular rhythm or groove seemed to escape me, no matter how hard I tried. But I learned to accept these problems as opportunities for growth, using them as fuel to push myself harder and to keep exploring.

Slowly but surely, I began to see progress. The once-challenging rhythms started to feel more familiar beneath my hands, the grooves and patterns becoming more fluid and natural. I could feel myself growing as a drummer, my passion for Indian music deepening with each passing day.

Looking back, I realise that this period of independent exploration was crucial to my development as a musician. It taught me the value of persistence, of pushing through difficult times and learning to find joy in the journey, even when the destination seemed far off.

More than that, it ignited a fire within me, a burning desire to keep learning, keep growing, and keep pushing the boundaries of what I thought was possible. And though I didn't know it at the time, this fire would soon lead me to a turning point in my musical journey, one that would change the course of my life forever.

Words of Wisdom
That Guided My Journey

"I fear not the man who has practised 10,000 kicks once, but I fear the man who has practised one kick 10,000 times." - Bruce Lee

Bruce Lee's quote about practice and commitment really speaks to me. As someone who has spent countless hours practising the drums, I know that true skill comes from focusing on the basics and repeating them over and over again. This quote inspired me to break down my practice into smaller steps and to give my full effort to each one. It has become a guiding principle for me, not just in music but in life, reminding me that greatness comes from consistent hard work and never giving up. - Pritish

3.2   Finding the Right Mentor: A Turning Point

As I continued to explore Indian music and drumming independently, my mother noticed the struggles I faced without proper guidance. She felt my pain and frustration and took it upon herself to find a solution. With a strong determination, she began researching potential mentors who could help me in my musical journey.

After months of tireless efforts, in Nov 2019, my mother finally found a renowned teacher, Drummer Sridhar based in Chennai, India, who offered online lessons. Although we were initially hesitant about the idea of online classes, my mother's instinct told her that this could be the turning point we had been looking for.

From the moment we reached out to him, he showed a genuine interest in my musical journey and a willingness to take me under his wing. He recognised my passion and potential in a trial class and agreed to take me on as his student.

Under his guidance, I began to make rapid progress in my drumming skills. He patiently taught me the correct techniques, helping me to unlearn the incorrect techniques I had picked up along the way and guiding me towards a more authentic and distinctive understanding of drumming.

His approach to teaching was unlike anything I had experienced before. He had a way of breaking down complex concepts and techniques into simple, easy-to-understand steps, making even the most challenging aspects of drumming feel accessible and achievable.

3.3 Overcoming Challenges and Unlearning Incorrect Techniques

As I went deeper into my lessons with my new mentor, I quickly realised that I had to confront and deal with the incorrect techniques I had unintentionally learned in my previous music schools.

Unlearning these incorrect techniques proved to be a painful and frustrating process. I had to retrain my muscles, break free from the patterns that had become second nature to me, and relearn the fundamentals of drumming from the ground up.

I remember the first few weeks of this process, the way my hands would ache after each lesson, the muscles protesting against the unfamiliar movements and positions. There were times when I would feel discouraged, wondering if I would ever be able to break free from these incorrect techniques that had taken root.

But my mentor's patience, encouragement, and continuous support helped me to keep going through these difficult times. He would remind me that growth often comes with discomfort and that the pain I was experiencing was a sign that I was making progress.

One particularly challenging moment came when my mentor introduced me to a complex drum pattern that he considered crucial for my development. As he explained the pattern, he said, "This is one of the most important patterns you'll learn, but it's also one of the hardest. Take your time to master it. I know you can do it. I believe in you."

The complexity of the pattern, combined with the pressure of my mentor's expectations, overwhelmed me.

I found myself struggling to hold back tears as I tried to wrap my head around the task at hand. Seeing my frustration, my Dad stepped in to help. He sat down with me and taught me a valuable lesson about breaking down complex problems into smaller, more manageable pieces. Together, we divided the drum pattern into smaller sections, focusing on mastering each part before putting them all together. With this new approach and my father's encouragement, I threw myself into practice with heightened determination. To my mentor's surprise and delight, I managed to master the complex pattern in just one week, far exceeding his initial one-month timeline.

This experience taught me a powerful lesson that extended far beyond drumming. I learned that even the most daunting challenges can be defeated by breaking them down into smaller, achievable goals. It was a valuable life lesson that I would carry with me, applying it not just to music but to every aspect of my life.

And so, I pushed through the frustration and the discomfort, focusing on the small victories and the moments of breakthrough. Slowly but surely, I began to feel the correct techniques becoming more natural, the once-painful movements flowing with greater ease and fluidity.

As I continued to work with my mentor, I began to understand the importance of proper technique, not just for the sake of playing correctly, but for the longevity and health of my body as a drummer. He taught me how to listen to my body, to pay attention to the signals it was sending me, and to adjust my playing accordingly. Within a span of two months, I went to the level of playing solo stage shows in Indian drumming.

Through this process of unlearning and relearning, I not only became a better drummer, but I also developed a deeper appreciation for the discipline required to truly excel in any craft. I learned that growth is not always a straightforward process and that disappointments are an inevitable part of the journey.

But I also learned that with continued effort, patience, and the right guidance, no hurdle is impossible to cross. And as I continued to work with my mentor, I could feel myself becoming not just a more skilled drummer, but a stronger and more adaptable one as well.

3.4 Unlocking Potential: Music as a Lifeline During the Covid-19 Pandemic

> *The right teacher is not just a source of knowledge but a guide, a mentor, and a partner in the pursuit of one's dreams. They have the power to shape not only our skills but also our character, instilling in us the values of hard work and determination that will serve us well throughout our lives.*

Just as I was getting used to my new drumming routine, the world was suddenly turned upside down by the COVID-19 pandemic. Like everyone else, my family had to deal with the lockdown situation, social distancing, and a completely new way of life.

At first, the sudden change to online school and not being able to go to my usual activities like karate, cricket, and swimming was confusing. But as I got used to the new normal, I quickly realised that the extra time at home was a chance for me to focus even more on music.

With my parents' support and encouragement, I decided to use the lockdown time to practice more. I went from my usual routine to spending 7-8 hours a day on drumming, splitting it up into smaller sessions with breaks in between. This intense practice helped me get a lot better at my technical skills and expressing myself through music.

During this time, we also started my YouTube channel, which was something we had been planning to do but never had the chance or know-how to do before. We had to learn a lot about making videos, posting them online, and getting people to watch them, but we were determined to make it work. We started posting drum covers and performances, slowly building up my online presence and connecting with people from all over the world who watched my videos. The positive comments and support from viewers gave me a huge boost of motivation and encouragement during the tough times of the pandemic.

One of the biggest things that happened during this time was how much closer I got with my drumming mentor from India. Even though we couldn't be in the same place, our online lessons became a regular part of my life, happening four times a week. This intense training not only helped me with music but also gave me a sense of stability and connection during the craziness of the pandemic. With his guidance, I went deeper into the world of Indian rhythms and techniques, growing my musical knowledge and skills.

The pandemic also made me realise just how powerful music can be in bringing people together and helping them heal. As the world faced the stress and worries of the crisis, I found that my drumming could bring joy, comfort, and emotional support not just to me, but to my whole family.

Music became our way of dealing with the hardships and worries of the pandemic. The positive energy from my practice sessions filled our home, creating a happy feeling that helped us feel normal and hopeful, even when the world around us was in chaos. My family's love, support, and shared experience of music kept us connected and strong, even as everything else seemed to be falling apart.

Plus, I realised that the good vibes from my music went beyond just my family. Through my YouTube channel and social media, I was able to share my passion and bring happiness to people around me who were also struggling with the pandemic. Knowing that my drumming could give someone a moment of joy, inspiration, or relief gave me an even bigger reason to keep working on my skills.

Looking back, I can see that even though the COVID-19 pandemic was super tough, it was also a major turning point in my music journey. The extra time and focus I put into practice, the growth of my online presence, and the stronger relationships with my teachers and family all came together to create a time of intense growth and change for me.

Through this experience, I learned how important it is to be flexible, open-minded, and able to find ways to grow even when things are really hard. I found out that with the right mindset and people supporting you, challenges can be turned into opportunities for positive change and personal growth.

3.5 Pursuing Trinity Exams: A Journey of Dedication

As my skills continued to develop under my mentor's guidance, my parents and I began to discuss the possibility of completing the Trinity drum grading exams. My mentor was supportive of this idea and encouraged me to work through the Trinity learning materials. Given my rapid progress and advanced skills, we thought it might be possible for me to take the Grade 8 exam directly, without going through the lower-grade exams.

When we shared this idea with my mentor, he expressed some concerns. He feared that the demands of the Grade 8 exam might prove too overwhelming for someone of my age and experience level, and he worried that it could potentially dampen my enthusiasm for drumming if I were to face disappointment or failure. Instead, he suggested that I take the lower-grade exam first, to familiarise myself with the exam pattern and manage the stress, before progressing to the higher grades.

Despite my mentor's reservations, my parents and I remained convinced that with the right preparation and support, I could rise to the challenge of the Grade 8 exam. My parents discussed this with my mentor, and we started the learning process with the Trinity system, and I had learned all the pieces and technical requirements for Grade 8. The extra time I gained due to the COVID-19 pandemic and lockdown allowed me to increase my practice hours drastically, further honing my skills and preparations. However, we needed more support from my mentor to prepare for the exams successfully. But I did not get that support from my mentor at this time, due to unforeseen circumstances. The sudden unavailability of my mentor left us in a state of shock and disappointment. It was an unfortunate situation, but we knew we had to keep moving forward. My mother, with her strong determination, refused to let this blocker deter us from our goals. She immediately started looking for a new teacher who could support my Grade 8 preparation for the Trinity exams.

After a period of intensive research and reaching out to various contacts in the music community, we found a highly skilled and experienced drum teacher who specialised in preparing students for the grading exams. He agreed to take me on as a student and help me work towards my Grade 8 goal.

I began attending weekly lessons with my new teacher, travelling for hours several times a week, to work with him. The journey was challenging, as balancing my regular schoolwork and my extracurricular activities alongside the demanding Trinity exam preparation required a great deal of effort, time management, and hard work.

Throughout this process, the steady support of my parents kept me motivated and focused. They helped me plan my practice schedule, ensuring that I had enough time to rest and recharge between intense sessions. They were there to encourage me during moments of self-doubt and to celebrate my progress along the way.

When the day of the exam finally arrived, I had to record my performance and submit it online to Trinity College London for evaluation. Despite the absence of a live audience, I still felt a touch of nervousness as I sat down behind my drum kit, knowing that this performance would be judged by experts in the field.

However, I channelled all of my passion, determination, and skill into my playing, pouring my heart and soul into every piece. A couple of weeks later, on 31st Dec 2020, we received the email with the results, and to my great joy and relief, I had passed the Grade 8 exam with Merit, and merely missed the distinction by a few marks!

This achievement was not just a testimony to my hard work, but also a reflection of the tireless support and guidance I had received from my parents, instructors, and everyone else who had believed in me along the way.

After this milestone, my former mentor engaged with us, reconnecting and expressing his pride in my accomplishment. While I was grateful for his support, I knew that my journey had taken me in a new direction. I wanted to continue growing in both Indian and Western music, so I decided to continue my music journey with my new instructor while

also resuming lessons with my former mentor to explore Indian music further.

Looking back, I realise that the most important lesson I learned through this experience was to trust my instincts and to have the courage to craft my path. With the right combination of passion, intent, and support, I now knew that I could get over any obstacle and achieve any goal I set my mind to. And with this newfound confidence, I looked forward to the next chapter in my musical journey, ready to take up all the opportunities in front of me.

CHAPTER 4

Exploring New Horizons

4.1 Discovering the Depths of Carnatic Vocals

As my musical journey progressed and my interest and skills in Indian music grew, my family and I decided, after much consideration and guidance from experienced musicians, that learning Carnatic vocals would be a valuable addition to my musical education. We believed that this would help shape my overall understanding and appreciation of music and complement my growing proficiency in Indian drumming.

Starting on this new path, we began searching for a suitable teacher who could guide me through the ins and outs of Carnatic music. The process of finding the right mentor was not easy, as we encountered several teachers who didn't quite meet our expectations or requirements.

However, after a period of trial and error, we finally connected with a highly skilled and experienced Carnatic vocal teacher based in Malaysia. Although the lessons would be conducted online, we felt a strong connection with this teacher and were impressed by their knowledge, passion, and teaching methodology.

Under the guidance of my new Carnatic vocal teacher, I began to explore the fascinating world of ragams, thalams, and the rich history of South Indian classical music. I was fascinated by the complex melodic patterns, the subtle variation of expression, and the deep spiritual and emotional connection that Carnatic music fostered.

As I went deeper into my lessons, I discovered that learning Carnatic vocals was not just about singing notes and rhythms; it was about understanding the very essence of the music, the bhavam (emotion), and rasam (aesthetic experience) that each composition sought to convey.

My teacher's patient and nurturing approach, combined with their vast knowledge and experience, helped me to navigate the complexities of Carnatic music with growing confidence and skill. I found myself eagerly looking forward to each lesson, keen to discover new layers of meaning and beauty within this ancient art form.

To my delight, I found that the skills and techniques I was learning in Carnatic vocals had a profound impact on my drumming as well. The sophisticated rhythmic patterns and the emphasis on improvisation and expression in Carnatic music began to inform my approach to drumming, allowing me to bring a new level of depth and modulation to my performances.

I started incorporating Carnatic rhythms and phrases into my drum practice, experimenting with ways to blend the two musical worlds. The results were exciting and deeply satisfying, as I felt I was not only growing as a vocalist but also expanding my horizons as a drummer.

As I continued to make rapid progress in my Carnatic vocal lessons, my teacher expressed her joy and amazement at my natural drive and ability. They encouraged me to keep pushing myself, to explore the vast ocean of Carnatic music with an open heart and a curious mind.

And so, with each passing day, I found myself falling more deeply in love with the beauty and complexity of Carnatic vocals, eager to see where this new path would lead me and how it would shape my overall musical journey.

4.2   Immersing in the Rhythm of Mridangam

My interest in Carnatic music took on a new dimension when I watched a fascinating movie about the mridangam, a traditional South Indian percussion instrument. The film, which chronicled the life and journey of a young mridangam prodigy, ignited a spark within me, and I found myself utterly fascinated by the instrument's rich history, complex techniques, and soulful tones.

Eager to explore the mridangam further, I approached my Carnatic vocal teacher and shared my newfound passion. To my delight, they were fully supportive of my interest and even offered to connect me with a renowned mridangam teacher, Vidvan Matheshwaran, who could guide me in my learning journey.

However, acquiring a mridangam proved to be a hurdle in itself. The instrument, which is made from Jackfruit wood and Buffalo skin, is subject to strict import regulations due to its natural materials. My parents spent weeks navigating the complex world of customs and shipping, determined to find a way to bring the mridangam into my life.

After much thought and patience, we finally managed to secure a beautiful mridangam, and I could hardly contain my excitement as I held the instrument in my hands for the first time. The weight of the wood, the texture of the skin, and the promise of the music waiting to be unleashed – it was a moment I will never forget.

Under the guidance of my mridangam guru, I began to delve into the nitty-gritty of the instrument. From the basic strokes and finger techniques to the complex rhythmic patterns and improvisations, I found myself utterly absorbed in the learning process.

The journey was not without its test and trials of course. The physical demands of the mridangam, the need for precision and strength in my fingers and wrists, and the mental acuity required to navigate the complex rhythms – all of these tested me in new ways, pushing me to grow not just as a musician but as a person.

But with each passing day, as I sat with the mridangam nestled in my lap, playing out the sounds and rhythms that had captured my heart, I felt a deep sense of connection and purpose. The instrument became an extension of my being, a channel through which I could express the depths of my emotions and my musical ideas.

As I continued to make progress in my mridangam lessons, I found that the skills and techniques I was learning were not only enhancing my understanding of Carnatic music but also enriching my approach to drumming, percussion, and music as a whole. The mridangam opened up new pathways of creativity and expression, allowing me to bring a fresh point of view and a deeper sense of rhythmic variations to all of my musical pursuits. And so, with each resonant stroke of the mridangam, I felt myself being drawn ever deeper into the rich world of Indian classical music, eager to explore the endless possibilities.

4.3 Unlocking the Harmony of the Keyboard

As I continued to immerse myself in the world of Carnatic music, both through my vocal lessons and my mridangam studies, my family and I began to realise the importance of having a well-rounded musical education. We understood that to truly excel as a musician, it was crucial to have a strong foundation in both melody and harmony and to be able to understand the depth of musical structure and composition.

With this in mind, and after much discussion with my music teachers and mentors, we decided that learning the keyboard would be an invaluable addition to my musical journey. The keyboard, with its ability to produce a wide range of sounds and its versatility in both Western and Indian classical music, seemed like the perfect instrument to bridge the gap between my various musical activities.

However, given our past experiences with finding suitable teachers, we knew that we had to be cautious and thorough in our search for a keyboard instructor. We wanted someone who could not only teach me the technical aspects of playing the instrument but also guide me in understanding the shades of both Western and Carnatic music.

After extensive research and numerous consultations, we finally found a highly recommended keyboard teacher, Mr. Balakrishnan, based in Coimbatore, Tamil Nadu, India. This teacher, who was well-versed in both Western and

Indian classical traditions, had a reputation for providing a holistic and immersive learning experience to his students.

As I began my keyboard lessons, I was immediately struck by the breadth and depth of knowledge that my teacher possessed. He not only taught me the fundamentals of playing the instrument – the scales, chords, and fingering techniques – but also helped me understand the underlying theories and concepts that governed both Western and Carnatic music.

Under his guidance, I began to explore the fascinating world of harmony, learning how to construct chords, understand progressions, and create beautiful melodies that could stand on their own or complement the rhythms of the mridangam and the vocals of Carnatic music.

I found that learning the keyboard not only enhanced my understanding of music as a whole but also opened up new avenues for creative expression and experimentation. I began to see how the skills and knowledge I was acquiring could be applied to my drumming, my vocal performances, and even to the creation of my original compositions.

As I went deeper into my keyboard studies, I discovered a profound sense of joy and contentment in the act of making music. The ability to express myself through the keys, to create harmonies that could evoke a wide range of emotions and experiences, was a revelation to me, and I found myself eagerly anticipating each lesson and practice session.

My keyboard teacher, with his patient guidance and steady support, helped me navigate the complexities of the instrument, always encouraging me to push myself further and explore the unlimited possibilities of music.

And so, as I sat at the keyboard, my fingers dancing across the keys, I felt a deep sense of gratitude for the opportunity to expand my musical boundaries, explore new instruments and traditions, and continue growing as an artist. I knew that the journey ahead would be filled with countless challenges, but with the support of my family, my teachers, and my passion for music, I was ready to face whatever was approaching, one note at a time.

4.4   Bringing Together Musical Traditions

As I continued to immerse myself in the study of Carnatic vocals, mridangam, and keyboard, I began to see how these seemingly distinct musical paths were, in fact, very well interconnected. Each discipline informed and enriched the others, creating a vibrant fabric of musical knowledge and experience.

My Carnatic vocal lessons taught me the importance of bhavam and rasam, of conveying emotion and sentiment through music. This understanding deeply influenced my approach to playing the mridangam and keyboard, as I sought to infuse my performances with the same depth of feeling and expressiveness.

Similarly, my mridangam studies heightened my awareness of rhythm and timing, not just in percussion but also in vocal music. I learned to anticipate and respond to the subtle rhythmic nuances of Carnatic compositions, my mridangam training informing my vocal phrasing and delivery.

Through my keyboard lessons, I gained a deeper appreciation for the harmonies and structures that underpin both Western and Carnatic music. This knowledge, in turn, enriched my understanding of the melodic and rhythmic elements I was learning in my vocal and mridangam studies.

As I wove these various musical threads together, I began to see the beauty and power of a holistic musical education. Each discipline, each instrument, and each lesson was like a different colour or texture, contributing to the vibrant world of my musical journey.

At the heart of this journey was a deep love and respect for the traditions and wisdom of Indian classical music. Through my studies of Carnatic vocals, mridangam, and keyboard, I was not just learning to play music; I was connecting with a rich cultural heritage, a legacy of artistic expression and spiritual devotion that stretched back centuries.

With the guidance of my teachers, the support of my family, and the passion that burned within my heart, I felt ready to accept whatever comes my way. I knew that as long as I approached my musical journey with faithfulness, humility, and an open heart, there was no limit to the growth I could achieve.

And so, with a sense of excitement and anticipation, I looked to the future, eager to see how the world of my musical journey would continue to unfold, weaving together the threads of tradition, innovation, and personal expression into a unique and beautiful work of art.

The Guinness World Record Journey

5.1 A New Challenge: Deciding to Break a Record

As my musical journey progressed and I continued to grow as a drummer, my parents began to explore new ways to showcase my skills and hard work. We had always been aware of Guinness World Records and the incredible feats people achieved, but we had never considered attempting one ourselves. That is, until one day when my mother suggested the idea of breaking the record for the most drum beats in a minute.

At first, I was fascinated but also scared by the prospect. I had no idea what the current record was or how to go about breaking it. But as we researched and discussed the possibility further, I began to feel a growing sense of excitement and determination. This was an opportunity to challenge myself in a new way, to push the boundaries of my abilities and see just how far I could go. Further, I was always fond of fast drumming.

My mother, ever supportive of my dreams and aspirations, encouraged me to take some time to think about the decision. She emphasised that breaking a world record would require a great deal of effort and patience. It was not a task to be taken lightly, but one that could ultimately help me grow as a musician and as a person.

I spent the next few days contemplating the idea, weighing the potential benefits and challenges. I knew that attempting a world record would be a significant undertaking, requiring months of intense practice and preparation. But the more I thought about it, the more I felt a deep sense of purpose and excitement. This was a chance to make my mark on the world, to achieve something truly extraordinary and to inspire others to pursue their dreams.

5.2 Discovering the Drumometer and Initial Attempts

One of the first challenges we faced in preparing for the Guinness World Record attempt was figuring out how to accurately measure and track the number of drum beats played in a minute. After some research, we discovered a specialised device called a Drumometer, which could count the beats in real-time when connected to a drum pad, and it's an approved device by Guinness World Records.

Excited by this revelation, we quickly ordered a Drumometer and eagerly awaited its arrival. When the package finally came, I couldn't wait to unbox it and start experimenting. I spent some time familiarising myself with the device, learning how to set it up and use its various features.

With the Drumometer ready to go, I sat down to make my first attempt at the record. I took a deep breath, focused my energy, and began to play as fast as I could, pouring all my concentration into maintaining a steady, rapid beat. But when I finished and looked at the Drumometer's display, I was shocked to see a count of just over 250 beats – a far cry from the world record of 2,109 beats at that time.

Disappointed but not discouraged, I realised that I had a long way to go before I could even come close to challenging the record. This initial attempt served as a reality check, highlighting the gap between my current skills and the level I needed to reach.

Over the next few weeks, I threw myself into training with new energy and excitement. I spent hours each day at my drum kit, working on techniques to increase my speed and endurance. I experimented with different grips and hand positions, seeking ways to optimise my movements and minimise wasted energy. Progress was gradual but steady, and my family celebrated each small victory along the way.

As I continued to practice with the Drumometer, I began to see my numbers climb – 600 beats, then 700, then 800. Each new milestone was a piece of evidence of the long hours and tireless effort I was putting in. But even as I celebrated these achievements, I knew that I still had a long way to go.

There were moments of frustration and self-doubt, times when the magnitude of the challenge felt overwhelming. But whenever I felt my resolve shattering, my parents would make me think back to the moment I first decided to pursue the record – the sense of purpose and possibility that had filled me. I would remind myself of the reasons why I had taken this in the first place – to push myself, to grow as a musician and a person, and to inspire others to chase their dreams.

And so, with a deep breath and a sense of determination, I would pick up my drumsticks and keep practising, keep pushing, keep believing. Through countless hours of sweat and struggle, through blisters and sore muscles and moments of pure exhaustion, I held onto my goal with steady focus and grit.

Looking back on those early days with the Drumometer, I realise now that they were laying the foundation for the incredible journey ahead. They were teaching me the true meaning of persistence that I had never imagined before, the importance of setting your sights high and working tirelessly to reach them. They were showing me that progress is rarely a straight line, but a series of ups and downs, breakthroughs and barriers.

But most of all, they were instilling in me a deep belief in my potential – the knowledge that with enough hard work and determination, I could achieve things I never thought possible. That belief would carry me through the ups and downs to come, all the way to the moment when I would finally see my name printed in the record books.

Words of Wisdom
That Guided My Journey

"I have not failed. I've just found 10,000 ways that won't work." - Thomas Edison

I love this quote from Thomas Edison. It reminds me of my own journey, especially when I was trying to break the Guinness World Record. There were many times when I wanted to give up, but this quote taught me that every mistake was a chance to learn and grow. It became my favourite saying, inspiring me to keep going even when things got hard. It showed me that success isn't about being perfect, but about using my failures to become better and stronger. - Pritish

5.3 The Long Road to the Record: Perseverance and Doubt

As the weeks turned into months, my Guinness World Record Journey became an all-consuming task, demanding every part of my physical and mental energy. I had settled into a rigorous training regimen, spending hours each day at my drum kit, pushing myself to the limits of my tolerance and skill.

The road to the record was a rollercoaster of highs and lows, all over the place. There were days when everything seemed to click, when I could feel myself getting closer and closer to that difficult-to-catch 2,109 mark. I would finish a session with my hands aching and my heart racing, but with a deep sense of satisfaction and progress.

But there were also days when, despite my best efforts, I would struggle to match my previous bests or see any significant improvement. It was frustrating, making me question whether I had what it took to break the record.

I remember one particularly tough period, several months into my training when I hit a wall that I just couldn't seem to break through. No matter how hard I practised, how much I pushed myself, my numbers on the Drumometer refused to rise. I could feel my motivation starting to shrink, doubt creeping in like a fog.

It was during this time that my mother, sensing my struggles, sat me down for a conversation. She asked me, with all the love and understanding in the world, if I wanted to take a break from the record attempt, to step back and perhaps try again in a year or two. She reassured me, saying,

"It's not a failure, it's not giving up, it's stronger to accept and move on to build strength if we know we don't have the capacity to do it now. Acceptance is braveness. It's okay to do so." For a moment, I was tempted. The thought of releasing myself from the pressure and the grind, giving myself rest to re-group, was incredibly appealing. But even as I considered it, I knew deep down that giving up was not an option. I had come too far, worked too hard, to back down now.

I looked my mother in the eye and told her, with a conviction that surprised even me, that I wanted to keep going. I wanted to see this through, no matter how long it took or how difficult it got. I knew that the only way to fail would be to stop trying, to let my doubts and my fears win out over my passion and my determination.

My mother, her eyes shining with pride and understanding, nodded and pulled me into a tight hug. She assured me that our family would be there to support me every step of the way, through every bit of the journey. She reminded me of how far I had already come, of the incredible progress I had made and the hurdles I had crossed.

With my new energy and my spirits lifted, I threw myself back into training with a renewed sense of purpose. I broke my practice sessions into smaller, more manageable chunks, focusing on quality over quantity and asked my mentor's guidance to enhance the techniques and practice drills. I started incorporating his advice alongside adding more rest and recovery time into my schedule, recognising the importance of giving my body and mind a chance to recharge.

Slowly but surely, I started to see progress again. My numbers on the Drumometer began to climb, getting closer and closer to that world record mark. Each small win felt like the greatest victory, a tribute to myself staying with power and patience.

And through it all, I had the strongest support and love of my family. They were my rock, my anchor, my constant source of encouragement and strength. They celebrated my successes, large and small, and helped me deal with my self-doubt and frustration. They believed in me even when I struggled to believe in myself, and their faith in my abilities never shattered.

Looking back on those long months of training, I am filled with a deep sense of gratitude and wonder. I realise now that the true reward of this journey was not just the prospect of breaking a world record, but the incredible growth and self-discovery that happened along the way. I was learning priceless lessons about the power within us to overcome seemingly unbeatable hindrances in life.

As I continued to train and prepare, my sights set firmly on the day of the official record attempt, I knew that regardless of the outcome, I would emerge from this experience a stronger, wiser, and more determined version of myself. This is what Mum always told me, the journey itself is a valuable learning experience, regardless of the result. I was ready to face whatever roadblocks were in front of me, armed with the knowledge that I had already achieved something remarkable simply by refusing to give up on my dreams.

5.4 The Day of Reckoning: Triumph and Disappointment

> *True focus and determination are not about rigidity or inflexibility, but about the ability to adapt and keep going ahead in the face of an ever-changing landscape – to stay locked in on one's goals while remaining open to new ideas, perspectives, and opportunities for growth. By nurturing a mindset of inextinguishable curiosity, humble self-awareness, and lifelong learning, we can navigate even the most turbulent waters with poise, purpose, and a strong commitment to our highest aspirations.*

The day of the Guinness World Record attempt arrived, and I woke up with a potent mix of excitement and nervousness. This was the moment I had been training for, the climax of countless hours of blood, sweat, and tears. I knew that everything I had worked for, every sacrifice and struggle, had been leading up to this important day.

As we arrived at the venue where the attempt would take place, I was struck by the gravity of the occasion. The space was buzzing with activity – cameras, lighting equipment, official timekeepers, and witnesses all in place to document and verify my performance. It was a fierce reminder that this was no ordinary drumming session, but a globally recognised test of skill.

I took my place on the throne, my hands trembling slightly as I adjusted my grip on the sticks. I could feel my heart beating fast in my chest, my breath coming in shallow bursts. But beneath the nerves, there was also a strong undercurrent of determination, focus, and confidence. I had prepared for this moment with every bit of my being, and I was ready to give it my all.

With a deep breath and a nod to the timekeeper, I began my first attempt. The Drumometer's display flickered rapidly as it counted each beat. I lost myself in the rhythm, my hands moving in a blur of speed and precision. For one intense minute, nothing existed except the beats, the drums, and the relentless vision of my goal.

As the final seconds ticked away and the timekeeper called time, I collapsed back onto my seat, my chest pounding. I had given it everything I had, pouring all my passion and skill into that minute of drumming. But when the official count was announced, my heart sank. I had fallen just short of the world record, my tally coming in a mere 40 beats below the 2,109 mark.

Disappointment washed over me in waves, and I could feel hot tears pricking at the corners of my eyes. After all the months of tireless practice, to come so close and yet miss the mark was a bitter medicine to swallow. For a moment, I felt like I had let myself down, let my family and supporters down.

But even amid my disappointment, I was surrounded by an outpouring of love and encouragement. My parents gave me a tight cuddle, their eyes shining with pride and admiration. They reminded me of my incredible performance and emphasised that this was not a failure, this was not the end of the world, but merely a stepping stone on the path to even greater achievements.

Sustained by my family's support and my determination, I resolved to try again. We scheduled a second attempt for a week later, giving me time to rest, reflect, and refine my approach. I went back into training with refreshed focus, analysing my performance and identifying areas where I could still improve.

On the day of my second attempt, I walked into the venue with a sense of calm clarity. The space felt familiar, and I was better able to navigate the setup. The nerves were still there, but they were tempered by a quiet confidence and a deep trust in my abilities. I had learned valuable lessons from my first attempt, and I was ready to apply them to this final shot at the record.

As I sat down behind the Drumometer and began to play, I could feel a difference in my performance. My movements were even more fluid and precise than before. The Drumometer's count climbed higher and higher, surpassing my previous best and getting ever closer to the world record mark.

In the final seconds of my attempt, I summoned every last bit of strength and focus, pouring my heart and soul into the drums. As the timekeeper called time, I knew in my bones that I had given it my all.

The room fell silent as I finished my final beat, the Drumometer's display facing the witnesses and the camera. I couldn't see the count myself, as the device was positioned for optimal recording, a requirement for the Guinness World Records' verification process.

Suddenly, the room filled with loud cheers and applause from my family, the witnesses, the timekeepers, and the sound engineer. I found myself surrounded by hugs and congratulations from everyone present. Tears of joy streamed down my face as I realised I must have broken the record, even though I didn't know the exact count yet.

My family, who had been intently watching the Drumometer, revealed to me that I had achieved an astonishing count of 2,370 beats, surpassing the previous Guinness World Record for the most drum beats in a minute. The reality of my achievement began to sink in, and I felt an overwhelming sense of pride and gratitude. All the hard work I had put into this goal had finally paid off.

In the days that followed, we compiled all the necessary paperwork, witness documents, and proofs required by Guinness World Records for validation. We sent the material to their headquarters, eagerly awaiting their official response.

On December 31st, 2021, exactly one year after receiving the incredible news of conquering my Trinity Grade 8 exam, another life-changing email arrived in my inbox. It was from Guinness World Records, officially confirming that I have set a new record for most drum beats in a minute at 2370 beats/minute. The timing felt like a beautiful coincidence as if the universe was aligning to celebrate my achievements and mark the beginning of a new chapter in my life.

As Mum read out the email loud, a mix of emotions flooded over me – joy, pride, disbelief, and an overwhelming sense of gratitude for all the support and love that had carried me to this moment. This tangible recognition of my achievement was proof of the incredible journey I had undertaken and the difficulties I had triumphed over. It represented not only the attainment of a dream but also the beginning of a new chapter in my life, one where I knew that with determination and hard work, anything was possible.

But more than that, I learned that no dream is too big, and no goal too scary when you have the love and support of those who believe in you. My family had been my rock throughout this entire journey, and their faith and encouragement had carried me through even the toughest of times.

As I looked out at the happy and proud faces of my loved ones, I knew that this moment of success was not just my own, but proof of the incredible power of a family with a common dream. And I knew that whatever challenges and opportunities came my way, I would face them with the same courage, wholeheartedness, and love that had brought me to this unforgettable milestone.

5.5 Lessons Learned: The True Meaning of Success

In the days and weeks following my successful Guinness World Record attempt, I found myself reflecting deeply on the incredible journey that had led me to that victorious moment. As the initial ecstasy began to settle, I realised that the true value of the experience lay not just in the achievement itself, but in the profound lessons I had learned along the way.

Perhaps the most significant of these lessons was the realisation that success is not always a linear path. There had been countless moments during my training when I had felt like I was stuck, when progress seemed slow or even non-existent. There had been difficulties and disappointments, days when the goal felt extremely far away.

But through it all, I had learned to trust in the process, to have faith that even the smallest steps forward were bringing me closer to my ultimate destination. I had discovered that true growth often happens in the quiet, unseen moments – the daily practice sessions, the incremental improvements, the refusal to give up even when the road ahead seemed the scariest.

Another crucial lesson I took away from the experience was the importance of finding ways to stay strong in the challenging times. Breaking a world record pushed me to my physical and mental limits, testing my determination and my ability to bounce back from disappointments.

I had learned that failure was not something to be feared or avoided, but an unavoidable part of any journey worth taking, as my Mum always reminds me of Thomas Edison's quote.

But perhaps the most important lesson of all was the realisation that no great achievement is ever a solo achievement. Throughout my journey, I have been blessed with the unshakeable love and support of my family, my friends, and my mentors. They had been my constant source of strength and encouragement, my safe haven in times of struggle and self-doubt.

I learned that we are all stronger, braver, and more capable when we are lifted by the belief and the love of others. My Guinness World Record may have had my name on it, but it was a tribute not just to my hard work and dedication, but to the incredible power of a loving family.

As I reflect on these lessons and the transformative impact they have had on my life, I am filled with a strong sense of gratitude and purpose. I now understand that the true meaning of success lies not in the award or the recognition, but in the person we become in the process of pursuing our passions.

Breaking a world record taught me priceless lessons about endurance, self-determination, and the power of believing in oneself. It has shown me that the greatest battles we face are often the ones within our minds – the self-doubt, the fear, the temptation to give up when the road gets tough.

But it has also taught me that when we dare to confront our inner demons, push past our perceived limitations, and keep working towards our goals, we unlock a potential within ourselves that knows no bounds. We discover a strength and a determination that can move mountains, can break even the strongest of barriers.

And I know that wherever my path may lead, I will always carry with me the memories of this incredible chapter in my life – the blood, sweat, and tears, the laughter and the love, the triumph and the transformation, for it was in following this dream that I discovered not just the depths of my potential, but the wonderful power of the human spirit to achieve the extraordinary.

CHAPTER 6

Rising Above: Dealing with Setbacks and Disappointments

6.1 The Media's Silence: A Test of Character

After the exhilaration of achieving the Guinness World Record, we were eager to share our accomplishments with the world. My parents reached out to various media outlets, hoping to spread the news of my achievement and inspire others with my story. However, what followed was a series of disappointments that taught me valuable lessons about self-worth, character, and the true meaning of success.

Despite our best efforts, most media showed no interest in covering my story. We contacted television channels, radio stations, and newspapers, but they were not showing much enthusiasm or interest. Some outlets politely declined, citing that my achievement, while impressive, did not align with their current focus or target audience. Others simply did not respond at all.

The reasons given for this lack of interest were disheartening. Some media representatives suggested that covering my story would not boost their ratings or revenue, implying that my accomplishment was not 'newsworthy' enough. It was a harsh realisation that the media often prioritise sensationalism and hype over genuine achievements and hard work.

Despite this disappointment, however, there was a light of hope and support from within my community. Local Indian magazines and radio stations recognised the significance of my achievement and reached out to conduct interviews and write articles about my journey. These platforms provided a space for me to share my story and connect with others who appreciated the value of hard work.

While the support from my community was heartening, the lack of recognition from mainstream media still weighed heavily on my mind. I couldn't help but question the fairness of it all – I had poured my heart and soul into achieving this record, and yet it seemed that my efforts were not valued by society at large.

Moreover, we couldn't help but wonder if my cultural background played a role in the media's indifference. As an Indian-origin child in Australia, I began to question whether my ethnicity had influenced their decision to overlook my story. It was a painful thought, but one that exposed the potential biases and inequalities that still exist in our society.

It was during this time of doubt and disappointment that my parents once again stepped in to offer their support and wisdom. They reminded me that true success is not measured by external validation or media attention, but by the personal growth and impact we create through our actions.

My mother helped me to reframe my viewpoint on the situation. She pointed out that while media recognition would have been nice, it was not the reason I had pursued the world record in the first place. I had set out on this journey to conquer myself, push the boundaries of my potential, and inspire others through my passion and dedication, all at a young age.

She also emphasised that the lack of media attention did not diminish the value of my achievement or the hard work I had put into it. The Guinness World Record was an endorsement of my commitment and skill, and that was something to be celebrated and cherished, regardless of external validation.

It was a difficult realisation for a young boy to grapple with, but through the guidance and wisdom of my parents, I began to understand that true success and happiness come from within. They taught me that external validation, while nice to have, should never be the driving force behind our goals and achievements.

I realised that the media's silence was not a reflection of my worth or the value of my achievement, but rather an opportunity for me to grow, develop a stronger sense of self, and find meaning and purpose in my objectives, independent of external recognition.

Instead, they encouraged me to focus on the intrinsic rewards of my musical journey – the joy of learning, the satisfaction of breaking barriers, and the personal growth that comes from chasing one's dreams wholeheartedly.

6.2 Finding Strength in Family and Inner Resolve

> *To anyone reading my story, I hope that it serves as a reminder that no dream is too big, no goal too audacious, when pursued with passion, commitment, and a strong belief in oneself. I hope that it inspires you to chase your own dreams recklessly.*
>
> *So to all the dreamers and the doers, the believers and the achievers – never give up on what sets your soul on fire. Never doubt the power of your own potential to change the world. And never, ever forget that with hard work, determination, and the love of those who lift you up, there is no limit to what you can achieve.*
>
> *Keep dreaming, keep striving, keep believing – and watch the wonder as the universe conspires to make your wildest dreams a reality. For that is the true magic of a life lived with passion and purpose – the magic of turning the impossible into the possible, one courageous step ultimately.*

As I navigated the complex emotions surrounding the media's lack of interest, I found comfort and strength with the constant support of my family. Their love, encouragement, and wisdom became a guiding light during this challenging time, reminding me of what truly mattered and helping me to maintain a positive stand in the face of disappointment.

My parents created a safe space for me to express my frustrations and doubts, listening with patience and empathy as I grappled with feelings of rejection and unfairness. They validated my emotions while also gently encouraging me to see the bigger picture and focus on the aspects of my journey that were within my control.

My father reminded me of the importance of staying true to oneself and one's values, even in the face of external pressures or disappointments. He encouraged me to focus on my personal growth and development, to find joy and satisfaction in the process of going after my passions, rather than seeking validation from others.

My mother, with her deep wisdom and insight, helped me to see the opportunity for learning and growth in every challenge. She taught me that true strength lies not in the absence of fear or doubt but in the courage to face those emotions head-on, to acknowledge them, and to keep moving forward despite them.

Through our deeply felt conversations, they shared their own experiences of facing discrimination, both in their personal and professional lives. They spoke explicitly about the hardships of being immigrants in a new country and the courage they had to cultivate to surpass the hardships and build a life for our family.

Together, my parents created a foundation of love, support, and understanding that allowed me to destroy the disappointment and emerge stronger and more determined than ever to pursue my dreams. Their stories were a powerful reminder that success often comes through purposefulness, self-belief, and a commitment to one's values, regardless of external validation or recognition. They taught me that true strength lies in rising above adversity, staying honest with oneself, and finding purpose in the search for one's passions.

Beyond the support of my immediate family, I also found strength in the broader network of loved ones and mentors who had been a part of my journey. My teachers, friends, and extended family members all played a role in lifting my spirits, offering words of encouragement, and reminding me of the value and significance of my achievements.

With my family's strong support and a new source of strength from within, I started to see the media's silence differently. Instead of seeing it as a big failure or a sign that I wasn't good enough, I saw it as a chance to prove to myself and everyone else that what mattered was not the quick flash of fame but the long-lasting power of my passion, my ability to bounce back, and my non-stop effort to be the best I could be and always growing as a person, no matter how tough the road ahead might seem.

Words of Wisdom
That Guided My Journey

"Believe you can and you're halfway there."
- Theodore Roosevelt

This quote from Theodore Roosevelt really hit home for me when I was dealing with the disappointment of not getting media attention after breaking the Guinness World Record. At first, I felt like my achievement didn't matter because no one seemed to care. But then I remembered this quote, and it reminded me that the most important thing was believing in myself and the value of my hard work. Even if others didn't recognise my success, I knew in my heart that what I had accomplished was incredible. Believing in myself gave me the strength to keep going and to find joy in my journey, no matter what anyone else thought.

6.3 The Power of Intrinsic Motivation and the Lessons Learned

As I reflected on the failures and victories of this period in my life, I began to develop a deeper understanding of the power of intrinsic motivation and the true meaning of success. The experience with the media's lack of interest, while painful at the time, once again it taught me valuable lessons about the importance of staying strong and confident at tough times.

It was during this time of reflection that I realised the profound impact my mother's teachings had on my life. From a young age, she had been nurturing my intrinsic motivation, encouraging me to pursue my passions and interests from a place of self-love and personal fulfilment.

I thought back to the incident when I first expressed my interest in playing the drums. My mother had asked me to take two weeks to reflect on my decision, to ensure that it was coming from a place of genuine passion and not just a passing fancy. At the time, I didn't fully grasp the significance of this lesson, but now, in the face of the media's indifference to my achievements, I began to see the wisdom in her approach.

My mother had been instilling in me the value of intrinsic motivation – the idea that true success and happiness come only from within. By encouraging me to focus on my self-worth, passions, and inner gratification, she had been helping me to develop a strong foundation of resilience and self-belief.

I realised that awards and recognitions, while tempting, can often lead to disappointment and unhappiness. When we tie our self-worth and happiness to the opinions of others, we give away our power and become vulnerable to unpredictable changes in life and often the biased world.

Instead, I learned to cultivate a strong sense of intrinsic motivation – to find joy and purpose in the act of going after my passions, rather than in the accolades or attention that may or may not come as a result. This shift in mindset was empowering, as it allowed me to take ownership of my happiness and success and to find meaning and satisfaction in the journey itself.

Moreover, the experience taught me valuable lessons about the realities of the world we live in – the biases, inequalities, and systemic barriers that can make it harder for some individuals to have their voices heard and their achievements recognised. It was a hard realisation, but one that also fuelled my determination to be part of the change I wished to see in the world. I wanted to show that success and excellence could come from anywhere and that with hard work and self-belief, anyone could achieve their dreams, regardless of their background or circumstances.

With this mindset, the lack of media recognition became a minor footnote in a much larger and more meaningful story – the story of a boy who dared to dream big, who faced his battles with courage and who found strength and purpose in following his passions.

Looking back, I am grateful for the lessons and growth that this experience brought me. It taught me that true success is measured by the impact we have on others, the character we develop through challenging situations, and the joy and fulfilment we find in chasing our dreams.

It also reinforced the importance of family, community, and the power of intrinsic motivation in achieving one's goals. I learned that with the love and support of those who believe in us, and with a strong sense of purpose and self-belief, we can overcome any obstruction and create our definition of success.

As I continue my musical journey, I carry these lessons with me, using them as a source of strength, guidance, and inspiration. I know that the road ahead will be filled with many more barriers, but I also know that I have the power and the support to face them head-on and emerge stronger and wiser on the other side.

And so, I embrace the journey, with all its ups and downs, knowing that each experience is an opportunity for growth, learning, and self-discovery. I may not always have the recognition of the mainstream media, but I have something far more valuable – the love of my family, the support of my community, and the strong belief in myself and my dreams.

CHAPTER 7

Expanding
My Percussive Horizons

7.1 Discovering the Marimba, Xylophone, and Timpani

> *In a world that is all too often marked by division, conflict, and suffering, music stands as a universal language of the heart, a reminder of our shared humanity and the unlimited potential within each one of us. By harnessing this power and sharing it with others, we can help to build a world of greater compassion and hope.*

As I continued to explore the vast world of percussion, my curiosity led me to discover a whole new array of instruments beyond the drums. The marimba, xylophone, and timpani captured my imagination, each offering unique qualities and expressive possibilities.

It was through a chance encounter with a young reporter, who interviewed me for the Indian Sun magazine after my Guinness World Record achievement, that I learned about these fascinating instruments. She had a background in percussion, and as we chatted about our shared passion for rhythm, she introduced me to the idea of expanding my percussive horizons.

Excited by the prospect of learning new instruments, I began to research the marimba, xylophone, and timpani. I was fascinated by the marimba's warm, resonant tones, the xylophone's bright, shimmering voice, and the timpani's deep, booming thunder. I listened to recordings of these instruments in various musical contexts, from classical orchestras to contemporary ensembles, and I knew I had to experience playing them for myself.

With the support of my family and as recommended by the reporter, we sought out a teacher who specialised in these instruments and could guide me in my exploration. That's how I met my new music teacher, Robert Oetomo, a renowned percussionist and educator who would become a pivotal figure in my musical journey.

From the first lesson with my percussion teacher, I was fascinated. He introduced me to the proper techniques for holding the mallets, striking the notes, and producing a range of dynamics and articulations. I was excited at the way the mallets danced across the marimba, creating melodies and harmonies that seemed to vibrate in the air. When I first struck the marimba with the mallets, the deep, resonant sound that filled the room sent a thrill through my entire body.

As I dived deeper into the study of these instruments, I discovered that each one had its unique challenges and rewards. The marimba demanded a keen sense of spatial awareness and proficiency as I learned to navigate its wide range of bars and produce smooth, fluid runs. The xylophone required a precise touch and careful control of the mallets to achieve its signature bright, crisp tones.

But beyond the technical aspects, I found that playing these instruments opened new avenues of musical expression and creativity. The marimba and xylophone allowed me to explore melodic and harmonic possibilities that the drums alone could not provide, while the timpani added a new dimension of depth and drama to my playing.

Under my teacher's guidance, I began to incorporate these instruments into my practice routine, exploring a wide range of repertoire, from classical transcriptions to contemporary works written specifically for percussion.

As I grew more comfortable with these instruments, I began to see how they could complement and enhance my drumming skills. The heightened sense of melody and harmony I gained from the marimba and xylophone informed my approach to rhythmic phrasing and musicality on the drum set. The timpani's demands for precise tuning and dynamic control helped me to develop a greater sensitivity to the subtleties of sound.

Through my exploration of these instruments, I felt my musical world expanding in ways I had never imagined. I was no longer just a drummer, but a percussionist in the truest sense of the word, capable of creating and shaping sound in a multitude of ways. And with each discovery, I felt a growing sense of excitement and possibility for where this percussive journey might lead me next. Little did I know that my newfound love for these percussion instruments would soon lead me to one of the most significant opportunities of my musical career thus far: the chance to audition for the prestigious Sydney Conservatorium of Music.

7.2 The Conservatorium Audition and Its Lessons

As my skills grew, my family and I began to discuss the possibility of taking my percussion studies to the next level as recommended by my teacher. We had heard about the Sydney Conservatorium of Music, a prestigious institution known for its rigorous programme and esteemed faculty, and we wondered if it might be the right place for me to continue my musical journey.

The reporter who had first introduced me to my percussion teacher and these other percussion instruments spoke highly of the Conservatorium and encouraged me to consider auditioning. She believed that the programme could provide me with the resources, guidance, and opportunities I needed to truly excel as a percussionist.

With a mix of excitement and nervousness, I decided to take the leap and prepare for the Conservatorium audition. I knew it would be a challenging process, requiring me to demonstrate a high level of proficiency on a range of percussion instruments and showcase my musical knowledge through aural and theory tests.

I threw myself into the preparation, dedicating long hours to improving my techniques, perfecting my audition pieces, and studying music theory concepts. My percussion teacher was an invaluable source of guidance and support throughout this process, helping me to refine my skills and build my confidence.

On the day of the audition, I arrived at the Conservatorium with all excitement buzzing through my body. As I walked into the audition room, I took a deep breath, centred myself, and began to play. I poured all of my passion and effort into each note and phrase, losing myself in the music and the moment.

When the audition was over, I felt a sense of pride and accomplishment, knowing that I had given my best effort and showcased the breadth of my percussion skills. I left the Conservatorium feeling hopeful and excited about the possibility of being accepted into the programme.

However, a few weeks later, when the results were announced, I was surprised and disappointed to learn that I had not been accepted. Instead, I was placed on the waitlist, which eventually turned out to be a no-spot that year. It was a difficult moment, one that forced me to confront the reality of rejection and the challenge of pursuing a competitive field like music.

But even in the face of this misfortune, I refused to let my disappointment diminish my love for percussion or my determination to continue growing as a musician. With the support of my family and teacher, I resolved to use the audition experience as a learning opportunity, a chance to reflect on my strengths and weaknesses and identify areas for improvement.

I realised that the Conservatorium audition had pushed me to new levels of excellence in my playing and that the skills and knowledge I had gained through the preparation process were valuable in their own right, regardless of the outcome.

Moreover, the experience once again reminded me of the important lessons about the ability to navigate failure and the importance of maintaining a growth mindset. I realised that rejection is not a reflection of one's worth or potential as a musician, but simply a part of the journey, an opportunity to learn, adapt, and come back stronger.

In the weeks and months that followed, I recommitted myself to my percussion studies with a new, energised focus. I continued to explore new repertoire, refine my techniques, and seek out opportunities to perform and collaborate with other musicians.

7.3 The Profound Influence of My Percussion Teacher

Throughout my journey as a percussionist, one of the most significant and transformative influences has been my percussion teacher. From the moment I first began studying with him, he has been a constant source of guidance, inspiration, and support, helping to shape not only my skills as a musician but also my character and outlook on life.

As a teacher, he possesses a rare combination of technical mastery, musical insight, and pedagogical skill. He has a deep understanding of the mechanics and modulation of each percussion instrument, and a gift for breaking down complex concepts and techniques into clear, accessible steps. Under his guidance, I have developed a solid foundation in the fundamentals of percussion playing, as well as a keen ear for tone, phrasing, and musicality.

But beyond his technical expertise, what sets him apart as a teacher is his ability to inspire and motivate his students.

He has a way of seeing the potential in each individual, of understanding their unique strengths and weaknesses, and of tailoring his approach to help them grow and succeed. He pushes his students to strive for excellence, but always with a spirit of encouragement and positivity, celebrating their progress and helping them to learn from their mistakes.

One of the things I admire most about him is his commitment to his growth and development as a musician and educator. Despite his many accomplishments and recognitions, he remains humble and committed to lifelong learning, always seeking out new ideas, techniques, and repertoire to share with his students. He models the values of curiosity, open-mindedness, and positivity that he seeks to instil in those he teaches.

But perhaps the most profound impact he has had on me extends beyond the realm of music. Through our lessons and conversations, he has become a mentor and a role model, someone who embodies the values of integrity, compassion, and service to others. He has taught me the importance of using one's talents and passions to make a positive difference in the world, and of being a good steward of the gifts and opportunities one has been given.

CHAPTER 8

The Balancing Act: Music, Life, and Perseverance

8.1 A Symphony of Pursuits: Embracing the Challenges and Joys

As I journeyed deeper into the world of music, exploring various instruments and genres, my life became a vibrant blend of my goals. Each new opportunity brought a sense of excitement and purpose, urging me to grow in ways I had never imagined. Yet, with this growth came the unavoidable problem of managing my time between all of the activities I enjoyed.

Alongside my musical aspirations, I was immersed in a rich array of activities that nourished my mind, body, and spirit. From the discipline and focus of karate to the fluidity and grace of swimming, from the strategic thinking of cricket to the academic rigours of school, each activity added a unique chapter to the ever-expanding journey of my life.

What struck me most about this array of activities was the way they complemented and enriched one another. The self-worth and confidence I cultivated through karate translated into a heightened focus in my music practice. The physical conditioning and breath control I developed through swimming enhanced my stamina and expressiveness on the drums. The strategic thinking and teamwork I developed on the cricket field sharpened my ability to collaborate and improvise with fellow musicians.

While I thoroughly enjoyed each of these activities, it would be a lie if I said that juggling so many passions was easy. As I progressed in each of these areas, I found myself not only growing in skill but also facing the important task of learning to manage my time. There were days when I felt stretched thin, my energy and attention divided among the various demands of my time. Long hours spent practising or studying took their toll, leaving me tired and occasionally overwhelmed.

However, it was through these tough situations that I learned some of the most valuable lessons of my journey. I learned to listen to my body and mind, to find moments to rest and relax in the middle of the hustle and bustle of my busy schedule. What kept me going, even in the toughest of times, was the greatest support and encouragement of my family. My parents were instrumental in creating an environment that allowed me to pursue my passions with full commitment and joy.

Through this multi-dimensional journey, I came to realise that true achievement comes not from a singular focus or achievement, but from the rich blend of experiences and connections that make up a life. Each target achieved, and each challenge overcome played an important role in shaping the person I was becoming and the path I was carving.

Central to this mindset was the idea that every activity I engaged in was something I genuinely enjoyed and found value in. Whether it was earning a new belt in karate, playing in my cricket tournaments, or executing a particularly challenging drum fill, I approached each task with a sense of curiosity, enthusiasm, and a desire to learn and improve. This positive outlook was reinforced by my family's steady support and the healthy habits they had instilled in me from a young age. Since the age of five, I have been waking up early, gradually adjusting my schedule to accommodate the increasing demands on my time. This discipline, coupled with a strong emphasis on mindfulness, healthy eating, and regular sleep, ensured that I had the energy and focus needed to tackle each day's tasks with energy and enthusiasm.

And so, as I navigated this exhilarating landscape of music and beyond, I did so with a sense of gratitude and wonder, knowing that every step, every note, every moment of difficulty and joy, was part of a greater symphony – the symphony of a life fully lived.

8.2 The Art of Balance: Wisdom from My Mother

As the demands of my various goals grew, particularly during the intense preparation for my Guinness World Record attempt, I found myself lost in the act of balancing my time and energy. It was during this period that my mother's wisdom and guidance became a beacon of light, helping me navigate the complexities of a passion-driven life.

From a young age, my mother instilled in me the idea that 'tomorrow never comes.' She emphasised the importance of living in the present, giving my all to each task at hand without worrying about the result, and not postponing my efforts or joy for an imagined future. This philosophy guided me through my early years, building a strong work ethic in making the most of every opportunity.

However, as I faced the mounting pressures of my Guinness World Record attempt, my mother introduced a complementary concept that, at first, seemed to contradict everything she had taught me before: 'There is always a tomorrow.' I remember feeling confused and unsure how to reconcile these two ideas.

With patience and wisdom, my mother explained that 'there is always a tomorrow' was not about putting off one's efforts or responsibilities, but rather about recognising that growth and success are ongoing processes. She helped me understand that every day brings new opportunities to learn, grow, and improve and that no matter how far we've come, there is always room for further discovery and refinement.

> *True balance is not about perfection or the absence of challenges but about the resilience to navigate life's ups and downs with grace, adaptability, and a strong commitment to one's values and aspirations. It is about embracing the journey, learning from the struggles, and finding joy and purpose in the pursuit of our passions, while always cherishing the love and support of those who matter most.*

As I began to grasp the delicate balance between these two concepts – the importance of living fully in the present while also embracing the ongoing nature of growth and learning – I developed a new frame of mind. I learned to approach each day with intentionality and purpose, to give my best in everything I do, but also to be patient and compassionate with myself, knowing that true mastery is a lifelong journey.

Through heart-to-heart conversations and her strong support, my mother helped me find my unique balance and rhythm. Her insights and encouragement were instrumental in helping me cultivate a mindset of presence, growth, and joy that would serve me well throughout my life.

8.3 The Power of Love and Support: My Family's Persistent Presence

As I reflect on my journey of integrating my musical aspects with the many other facets of my life, I am filled with an overwhelming sense of gratitude for the deepest love and support of my family. They were the bedrock upon which I built my dreams, the haven to which I could always return, and the guiding light that helped me navigate even the darkest and most challenging of times.

My parents were an inexhaustible source of strength, wisdom, and encouragement. They created a home environment steeped in love, laughter, and a deep appreciation for the power of chasing one's passions. From the moment I first expressed an interest in music, they were there to nurture and support my growth, providing not just the practical resources I needed, but also the emotional support and understanding that are so important to any creative journey.

My mother spent countless hours listening patiently as I practised my drums, offering words of encouragement and constructive feedback. She had an unimaginable ability to sense when I was feeling overwhelmed or discouraged and always seemed to know just the right thing to say to help me reframe my standpoint and find motivation.

My father was a constant pillar of support, working tirelessly to provide for our family and ensure that I had every opportunity to pursue my dreams. Despite the long hours he put in at work, he always made time to attend my performances, celebrate my successes, and offer a listening ear and a comforting hug when I needed it most.

Beyond their contributions, what struck me most was the way my parents worked together as a team, creating an admirable united front of love and support. They modelled for me what it means to be true partners in life – to support and uplift one another, to communicate openly and honestly, and to always put the needs and well-being of the family first.

There is another important person in my journey who I never spoke about. It's my little sister, Shreya. From the moment she entered our lives, she became an integral part of my world, a constant source of love, strength, and inspiration that would shape my journey in ways I could never have imagined.

Our bond began long before she even entered this world. My mother often tells me how, when she was pregnant with my sister, she would feel her kicks very strongly only in response to the sound of my voice. It was like even in the womb, my sister knew that I would be her forever friend. However, five years younger than me, her unlimited energy, infectious laughter, and unconditional love were a constant reminder of the pure joy and beauty that life has to offer, even during difficult situations.

As she grew, my sister became my shadow, always eager to be by my side, to share in my joys and my sorrows. From the day she started crawling, she would follow me around the house, her eyes wide with wonder and admiration. My mother would often joke that I was her alarm clock, for she would always wake up just in time to greet me when I returned home from school, her face lighting up with a smile that could melt even the toughest of hearts.

During the intense preparation for my Guinness World Record attempt, my sister's presence became the light that guided me through the long hours of practice and the moments of self-doubt. Though she was still too young to fully grasp the significance of what I was attempting, she seemed to understand instinctively that I was pouring my heart and soul into something deeply important to me.

She would sit with me for hours as I practised, watching the numbers on the Drumometer climb higher and higher. She would cheer me on with a fierce intensity, her eyes sparkling with pride and excitement every time I hit a new milestone.

She would often bring me water and snacks during my long practice sessions, insisting on being my 'official assistant' and making sure I was taking care of myself. And when frustrations and doubts would creep in, as they inevitably did during such a demanding time, she was always there with a hug, a smile, and a strong belief in my abilities.

But my sister's support extended far beyond just her physical presence. She had an unimaginable ability to sense when I needed a break when the pressure of my aspirations threatened to overwhelm me. In those moments, she would grab my hand, inviting me to play, to laugh, to experience the simple joys of being alive.

No matter what she was doing, whether it was creating her little masterpieces with her art supplies or exploring the world with her abundant curiosity, she would drop everything in an instant to be by my side. Her love and devotion were a constant reminder that, no matter how hard the situation may seem, I was never alone.

Even on the day of my Guinness World Record attempt, when the pressure was at its highest, her presence gave me the courage to keep myself grounded. When the final seconds ticked away, it was my sister's face that I sought out first in the sea of congratulatory hugs and well-wishes. Her joy and pride were unimaginable, her excitement infectious as she ran around the studio, celebrating my success with a purity of emotion that only a little child could possess.

At that moment, as I watched her revel in my accomplishment, I was struck by the deepest realisation. Through her innocence and love, my sister taught me one of the most valuable lessons of my life: that true happiness and contentment come not from external validation or recognition but from the love and belief of those who matter most.

In many ways, my sister is the unsung hero of my story. She is more than just a sibling; she is my confidante, my cheerleader, my partner in crime, and my forever friend.

As I sit here now, reflecting on all that I have experienced and all that lies ahead, I am reminded of the true essence of my journey – it is not just a story of personal growth and musical accomplishment but evidence of the transformative power of love and family. My parents and my sister were the melodies that underlay every note I played, the rhythm that propelled me forward, and the harmony that made my life's journey a true work of art.

And so, as I continue to navigate my beautiful life, I do so with a heart full of love and a spirit fortified by the steady support of my incredible family. They are my source of strength, my inspiration, and my greatest blessing, and I will carry their love and lessons with me always, no matter where my path may lead.

CHAPTER 9

Looking Ahead: Anticipating Future Challenges and Opportunities

As a 14-year-old, I am aware that my teenage journey has only just begun. While I have already faced and learned from my past, I know that there will be many more hurdles and opportunities waiting for me in the years ahead.

Looking forward, I anticipate that the digital landscape will continue to evolve at a rapid pace, presenting new distractions, pressures, and potential pitfalls. As technology becomes increasingly integrated into every aspect of our lives, it will be more important than ever to maintain a healthy balance and to use these tools in ways that support rather than hinder my personal growth and well-being.

I also recognise that as I progress through my teenage years, the academic and social pressures I face are likely to intensify. With the looming hurdles of high school, college admissions, and the increasing complexity of relationships and social dynamics, I will need to draw upon the lessons and strategies I have learned so far to stay focused, grounded, and true to myself.

At the same time, I am excited about the many opportunities that the future holds. As my musical skills continue to grow and evolve, I look forward to exploring new genres, collaborating with other artists, and using my platform to make a positive impact on the world. I am also eager to take on new battles in other areas of my life, whether it be through academics, extracurricular activities, or personal projects.

While I know that the road ahead will not always be smooth or easy, I feel better prepared to endure any trials, thanks to the experiences and lessons I have gained so far. I have learned the importance of setting clear goals, breaking them down into manageable steps, and celebrating progress along the way. I have also learned the value of seeking support and guidance when needed and of surrounding myself with people who uplift and inspire me.

Moreover, I have come to understand that problems are not barriers to be broken but opportunities for growth and self-discovery. By embracing a growth mindset and viewing failures as stepping stones to success, I believe that I can continue to learn, adapt, and evolve in the face of any tough situation.

As I look to the future, I am filled with a sense of hope, excitement, and determination. I know that the teenage years will bring their share of ups and downs, but I am confident in my ability to navigate these experiences with patience, wisdom, and grace.

I am grateful for the strong foundation that my family, mentors, and experiences have provided me so far, and I am committed to building upon this foundation as I continue to grow and discover new aspects of myself and the world around me.

While I may not have all the answers to all the problems that lie ahead, I know that I have the tools, the support, and the mindset needed to face them head-on. I am excited to see where this ongoing journey of self-discovery, growth, and transformation will take me, not just in my teenage years but in all the years to come.

So as I stand on the verge of this new chapter in my life, I do so with a sense of clarity, purpose, and anticipation. I am ready to face the exciting adventures that the future holds, to learn from my mistakes and celebrate my successes, and to continue becoming the best version of myself.

And so, as I step into this new chapter of my life, I do so with a heart full of hope, a mind full of ideas, and a soul ready to take up all the beauty and possibilities that music has to offer. I am excited to continue learning and growing, both as a musician and as a human being, and to use my gifts to make a positive impact in whatever way I can.

To all the aspiring musicians out there,

I want to say this: never underestimate the power of your passion and your unique voice. You have within you the ability to change lives, touch hearts, and make the world a more beautiful, compassionate place through your music.

So keep practising, keep dreaming, and keep believing in the transformative power of music. Together, let us create a future where every note, every melody, and every rhythm is a celebration of the human spirit – a testament to the beauty and the limitless potential that lies within us all.

My Pillars of Strength

My musical journey would not have been possible without the love, support, and encouragement of my family. They have been my pillars of strength, my guiding light, and my source of inspiration every step of the way. I am forever grateful for the sacrifices they have made to help me pursue my dreams. This book and all my achievements are dedicated to them, for they are the foundation upon which my success has been built.

In Praise of My Mentors

I am forever grateful to my incredible teachers who have guided me on my musical journey. They have not only shaped my skills as a musician but also my character and outlook on life. Each of them has generously shared their wisdom, knowledge, and passion, helping me grow not only as a musician but also as a person. Through their words, you will gain insight into the experiences and moments that have defined our teacher-student relationships. Join me in celebrating and honouring these remarkable mentors who have left an indelible mark on my life.

Drummer Sridhar
Drum Fighters Academy

Pritish is, without a doubt, one of my best students. His love for music is clear in everything he does. When he joined my academy at just 9 years old, I could see right away how passionate and interested he was in learning the drums.

What really sets Pritish apart is his amazing memory and his drive to practice on his own, without anyone telling him to. I would teach him really tough patterns and grooves, the kind that would be hard even for older students, but he would always take on the challenge with a big smile. He gives 100% to everything he does and has this inner fire that pushes him to win over any obstacle.

In every class, Pritish shows just how much he cares about music. Anything I teach him, he practices until he's mastered it and can show me in the very next lesson. His dedication and memory are truly special.

When Pritish was only 10, he shocked me by passing the tough Trinity College London Grade 8 exam with flying colours, and he did it with just a few months of practice. This is something that's hard even for drummers who have been playing for years, but Pritish made it look easy.

It's these amazing qualities - his love for music, his enthusiasm, and his positive attitude - that helped Pritish break the world record for the most drum beats in a minute when he was just 11. This incredible achievement got his name in the famous Guinness Book of World Records.

More than just his skills on the drums, what I really admire about Pritish is his happy and focused approach to learning. I always tell him that being happy and smiling is the key to learning music easily, and this comes so naturally to him.

Pritish is a true inspiration, and I feel lucky to be a part of his musical journey. His passion and hard work are unmatched, and I know he's going to do big things in the future. The world needs more people like Pritish, who have the courage to follow their dreams and the talent to make them a reality.

***

Pritish has been learning mridangam from me for the last four years, and I've been amazed by his natural talent from the very start. It's like music is a part of who he is. Whenever I teach him something new, he picks it up so quickly and easily.

In our lessons, Pritish has mastered some really challenging rhythms and techniques, like Adithalam, Roopagathalam, Misarachapu, and Kandachapu. And the best part? If I ask him to play anything from these, he does it without missing a beat. It's incredible to watch him in action.

K.Matheshwaran
Kanchi Kamakoti Peetam
Asthana Vidwan

What's even more impressive is that Pritish is a true multi-talented artist. He doesn't just play the mridangam; he's skilled at so many different instruments. It's rare to find someone with such a wide range of musical abilities.

Out of all my students, Pritish is definitely one of my favourites. He's not just talented; he's also a joy to teach. His passion for music shines through in every lesson, and it's an honour to be a part of his journey.

As Pritish continues to grow, both as a musician and as a person, I know he's going to achieve great things. I can easily picture him playing on big stages, sharing his incredible talents with the world. No matter where his musical path takes him, he'll always have my support and blessings.

Pritish is an exceptional young boy with a bright future ahead of him. I feel lucky to be his teacher and to witness his growth firsthand. I do not doubt that he's going to make a big impact in the music world, and I can't wait to see all the amazing things he'll accomplish.

***

Pritish is a truly multi-talented aspiring musician, excelling as a drummer, percussionist, and piano and electronic keyboard player. His resolve to mastering multiple instruments is evident in his pursuit of further grades in electronic keyboard and piano.

Bhuvarahan Balakrishnan
Chords and Swaras
Musical Institute

As Pritish's electronic keyboard and piano teacher, I am constantly amazed by his ability to absorb and apply new concepts quickly. He is a hardworking student who picks up lessons and songs with ease, demonstrating flawless execution in subsequent classes. His regularity and commitment to attending classes are commendable, reflecting his passion for music.

What sets Pritish apart is not just his talent, but also his humble and sincere nature. Despite his incredible achievements, including holding a Guinness World Record, he remains grounded and dedicated to his craft. This combination of skill and character is truly rare and speaks volumes about his potential for success.

I believe that Pritish's musical journey is just beginning, and I am excited to see where his path will lead. With the right guidance, exposure, and opportunities, he has the potential to become a globally recognised artist, inspiring audiences around the world with his passion and talent.

It is a privilege to be a part of Pritish's musical education and to witness his growth as a musician. I am confident that he will continue to make great strides in the music industry, and I look forward to celebrating his future successes. With his talent and the strong support of his family, there is no limit to what Pritish can achieve.

***

As a percussionist with global experience, I have had the privilege of teaching and mentoring many talented students throughout my career. However, Pritish stands out as a truly exceptional individual, not only for his inborn musical abilities but also for his loyalty to the craft.

Robert Oetomo
Percussionist & Composer

From the moment Pritish began studying with me, I recognised his extraordinary potential. His natural talent was evident in the way he quickly grasped complex rhythms and techniques, demonstrating a level of skill and understanding far beyond his years. But what truly sets Pritish apart is his insatiable curiosity and his willingness to explore the vast world of percussion.

Under my guidance, Pritish has delved into a wide range of percussion instruments, from the marimba and timpani to the xylophone and beyond. His ability to master these instruments with ease is a clear sign of his versatility and adaptability as a musician. He approaches each new challenge with enthusiasm and determination, always striving to push the boundaries of his own abilities.

I am particularly inspired by Pritish's openness to diverse musical styles and traditions. He welcomes the opportunity to learn from different cultures, incorporating elements of world music into his own playing. This global perspective will undoubtedly serve him well as he continues to grow and evolve as an artist.

Beyond his musical talents, Pritish possesses a rare combination of humility, gratitude, and devotion. He is always eager to learn and to refine his skills through diligent practice. His success is not just a result of his natural abilities, but also a reflection of his steadfast commitment to his craft.

It is a joy and an honour to be a part of Pritish's musical journey. I am sure that he will continue to achieve great things, not only as a percussionist but also as a well-rounded musician and individual. With his talent and hard work, Pritish has the power to inspire and touch the lives of many through his music.

As his teacher, I am excited to witness the heights he will undoubtedly reach, and I am committed to supporting and guiding him every step of the way. The world of music is truly fortunate to have a rising star like Pritish, and I am confident that his contributions will leave a lasting mark on the global percussion community.

***

The Rhythm of Resilience

15 Inspiring Tips to Help You Overcome Challenges and fuel your success.

- Trust in yourself and your dreams, no matter their size.

- View challenges as growth opportunities.

- Persevere through hardships and stay committed to your passions.

- Surround yourself with supportive people who believe in you.

- Find joy and purpose in the journey, not just the outcome.

- Celebrate your achievements, big and small.

- Stay humble and open to learning.

- Cultivate resilience and a positive mindset.

- Believe in the power of hard work and dedication.

- Use your unique story to inspire others.

- Your background does not define your future.

- Stay focused on your goals while enjoying the present.

- Success is about personal growth and satisfaction.

- Use your talents to make a positive impact on the world.

- Never stop dreaming and pushing boundaries.

www.ingramcontent.com/pod-product-compliance
Lightning Source LLC
Chambersburg PA
CBHW021555150726
47990CB00006B/2556